SHOULD I SELL MY STOCKS NOW?

SHOULD I SELL MY STOCKS NOW?

Why, When, and How Investors Should Sell, Hedge, or Short the U.S. Stock Market in 2020

CHRISTOPHER WESTFIELD

SHOULD I SELL MY STOCKS NOW: WHY, WHEN, AND HOW INVESTORS SHOULD SELL, HEDGE, OR SHORT THE U.S. STOCK MARKET IN 2020

Copyright © 2020 by Christopher Westfield, PiggyBankMedia

All rights reserved.

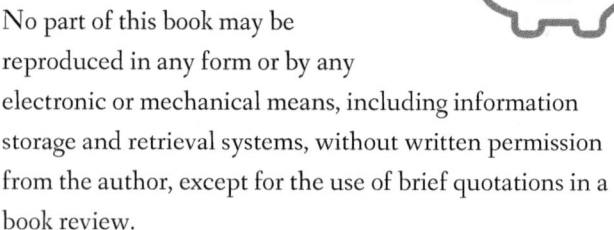

No part of this book may be reproduced in any form or by any electronic or mechanical means, including information storage and retrieval systems, without written permission from the author, except for the use of brief quotations in a book review.

DISCLAIMER: *This information contained in this book is for informational purposes only and should not be considered investment or professional advice of any kind. Consult with finance professionals and/or your own advisers before making any trading or investment decisions.*

First published in the United States of America by PiggyBankMedia.

Version: 1.1 [2/2020]

10 9 8 7 6 5 4 3 2 1 0

ISBN: 978-1-65396-029-3

Dedication

This book is dedicated to my phenomenal wife and amazing daughter who gave me the space, encouragement, and motivation to write it. Your unconditional love is priceless and it fuels me every day.

Contents

1. The Sell-Off — 13
   What I See Coming
2. My Investing Education — 27
   How I Got Here
3. HOW THIS BOOK IS ORGANIZED — 33
   Before We Get Started
   - Let's discuss 'WHY' — 34
   - Let's talk about 'WHEN' — 35
   - Let's discuss 'HOW' — 37
4. THE WHY? — 41
   Why Should I Get Out?
   - Here's My "WHY" — 42
   - Tax Sellers — 44
   - The REPO Liquidity Scare — 44
   - Weakness of Earnings — 46
   - The American Political Climate — 49
   - Serious Geopolitical Risks in 2020 — 52
   - Technical Indicators of a Correction — 53
   - Looming $1.6T Student Loan Debt Crisis — 57
   - Opinions From Some People I Respect — 57

5. THE WHEN? — 59
When Should I Sell, Short, or Hedge?

- The January Effect — 61
- Coronavirus COVID-2019 Timetable — 62
- Geopolitical Timetable — 63

6. THE HOW? — 65
What Strategies Should I Use?

- Short- and Medium-Term Spending Needs — 66
- Work-Based Retirement Plans — 67
- Technology Stock: Trading Example Using ETFs and Options — 71
- Options Trading Strategies — 76
- ETFs and Inverse-ETFs; Leveraged ETFs — 76
- Assets Not Correlated to US Markets — 77

7. MORE EXAMPLE TRADES — 81
Covering Other Possible Scenarios

- Other Trading Ideas in Down Markets — 87

8. Final Thoughts — 91
Always Remember Why You're Investing

- Acknowledgments — 97
- Author's Notes — 99
- About the Author — 105
- NOTES — 107
- STRATEGIES — 109

SHOULD I SELL
MY STOCKS NOW?

ONE

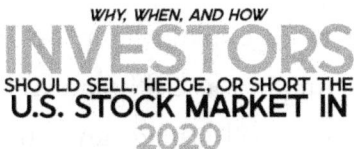

The Sell-Off

WHAT I SEE COMING

> "You get recessions, you have stock market declines. If you don't understand that's going to happen, then you're not ready, you won't do well in the markets."
>
> - Peter Lynch

WE'RE GOING DOWN IN 2020. I'm not saying that just because we've been going higher for so long. It's more that the serious market headwinds are out there, and by my estimation they're getting much, much stronger.

I wrote this short book because of a number of factors that I'll explain later, but I see a **big sell-off** coming in the US financial markets: the S&P500, Dow 30, Nasdaq, and the Russell in 2020. I've told my friends, family, and business associates to consider what this could mean for their money and assets in the near future, and whether this is a major hazard for them or an opportunity.

And since the commonly-accepted wisdom is that three out of every four stocks move with, and in the direction of the entire market, not many securities or sectors will be immune if we have a big pullback. And depending on whom you ask, we're due for a healthy correction anyway.

For your information, a correction in a stock, or an index, is a pullback of at least 10% from a high point. Historically, average corrections in the S&P 500 have been about down 13% and they last roughly four months.

But I think we could sell off harder than that.

What you just read—those opening six paragraphs—was the initial case I was making about the markets before all of this Coronavirus, 2019-nCoV, or COVID-19 activity started.

The bearish factors in play in our markets were already far-reaching and impactful, without the added confusion, drama, and turbulence of a viral outbreak in China, that developed into an epidemic, and depending on certain factors now widely accepted, this global pandemic.

Whatever happened in the central city of Wuhan, China and their animal 'wet markets,' I can't begin to understand —either as a consumer, or in the science behind the transmissions.

All I know is that as I write this, millions of citizens all around our globe are under lockdown, federally-mandated quarantine, and/or self-quarantine. Some have said that it's nearly 10% of the world's population in those three categories.

As an aside, I certainly hope it's a flu that our best scientists can conquer in short order, and that it's not the accidental release of a man-made laboratory virus, or bio-weapon, as some online have been speculating.

At this point, beyond the tens of thousands infected in China at this point, the spread to countries like South Korea, Japan, Iran, Hong Kong, and Italy are the outbreaks that are concerning to the whole world. Why? Because they show that while it is still without a cure or vaccine, this virus is easily spread and the containment measures have not been as effective as once thought.

Even though coronavirus has been included in regular discussions on financial networks in the USA like CNBC and Bloomberg— the stock markets have largely taken the drama, illnesses, and deaths in stride. That's until the move to both Iran in the Middle East and Italy in Europe has warned the markets about the scope of this growing problem.

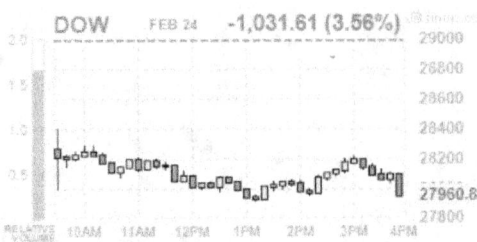

This is what DOW down a thousand points looks like. (February 24, 2020)

But without becoming a mad off-the-grid "prepper," (someone who 'prepares' for 'STHP' or 'sh$t to hit the fan,' as it were) I can already see that this could get much worse for our society before it gets better.

What does that mean for you, your loved ones, your financial stability?

Well, imagine the impact on life—all around the world—if communities, cities begin to lock down and 'shelter in place' to ride out this virus. Without forgetting the sad and horrific loss of life that have would precede such a situation, imagine the impact on goods and services, productivity, and all things related to our economy.

Okay, okay. Scary, so now I'll play devil's advocate with myself now and take the other side:

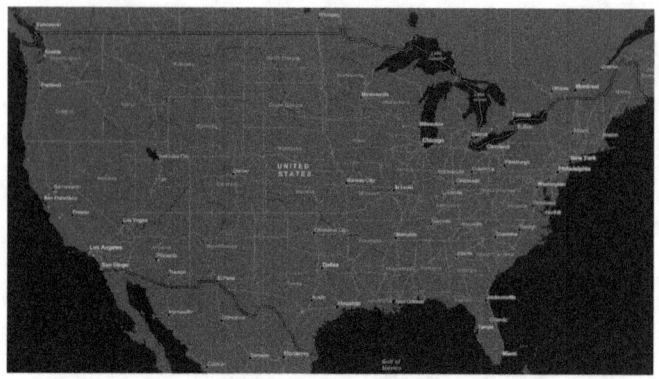

The current location of the thirty-five (35) confirmed cases of Coronavirus (2019-nCoV; COVID-19 virus) in the US from publicly available data at Johns Hopkins University / Baltimore, Maryland as of 2/23/2020 at 2:27pm.

Let's assume a few months out, the lockdown in China, and in other places across Asia, Europe, and elsewhere has worked and that the United States is spared the brunt of the virus. Even with our large population, imagine if the number infected (and the fatality rate) are kept quite low by the sheer will of our science, vigilance, strict quarantines, and our modern system of healthcare providers and first responders. Well, that would be great. Best case scenario, I'd say.

But even with this scenario, how many American businesses would be affected by global supply chain disruptions based on Chinese (or pan-Asian) manufacturing. There are even critical raw materials for products Americans regularly buy from places around the world that are made in China.

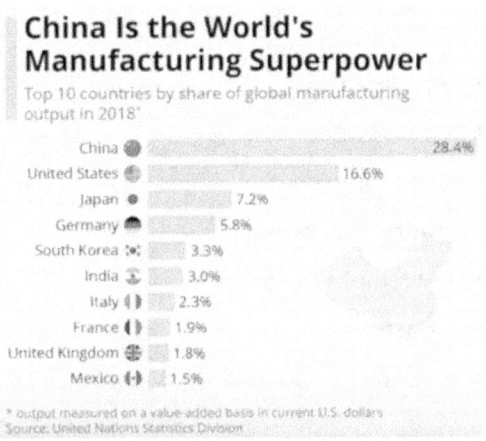

What does a global supply chain look like in 2020 and 2021 if China, Japan, South Korea, and Italy are under some extended quarantines?

Technology companies like Apple have already been able to underscore the impact to their earnings of a slowdown in global manufacturing: *If their products are not produced, they obviously can't be sold to consumers.* It's that simple. And while some analysts to think those profits will only be delayed, there is no guarantee of a future sale if changes occur in the consumer market.

For the entire technology sector, this is a big problem in 2020. How will lockdowns, extended social distancing, and quarantines impact these consumer products, many that come out of Asia?:

- televisions
- video game consoles
- smartphones
- smart speakers
- notebooks/laptops
- smart watches...
- and many more...

And how does that impact retailers (Target, Walmart, Amazon, etc) and shipping (Fedex, UPS, DHL, etc). We're completed interconnected to the manufacturing facilities in southern China and throughout Asia. If they stay offline even for a few months, there's no telling what the global economic impact will be. (Some are already estimating the losses globally could reach a trillion dollars: $1T or $1,000,000,000,000.)

And whether you ultimately agree with me or not, I appreciate you giving me the chance to share with you what I see as the many risk factors for our financial markets. After that, it's up to you what you want to do with this information—also because it's not meant to be investment advice of any kind. But since my perspective has cost you less than buying me a caffe latte (venti!) and a cream cheese bagel, you won't have risked much even if you decide not to react to any of these market conditions.

Whether you're reading this book in February 2020, during the spring, over the summer, or even late fall, I'm hoping this content provides a roadmap that gives you some strategies to either protect the investments you're holding long, or just helps you make some money (gains) to offset any losses (realized or unrealized) you'll take in a downtown.

I'll try to keep this book *lean and mean*, largely just my observations and my own strategies, and I promise to keep the filler out. But first, I will give you some idea of my trading/investing philosophy (SPOILER ALERT: *It's logical stuff I learned from my grandfather*), but after that it will be about the risks I see, and what I'll be doing about them. Remember, there's serious money to be made when volatility rules the markets. If we're prepared, we can do well.

Personal finance books like this are often written by **perma-bears**: those investors, traders, or short-sellers who always believe that the sky is falling. (In case you don't know, it's short for *permanent bears* and is the opposite of a *perma-bull*, a trader or investor who is perpetually bullish.) Perma-bears don't trust economic prosperity for more than a brief period, and they're generally pessimistic about all things financial. They seem to always be waiting for a recession in the market, or worse, a depression.

That's not me.

Over the years, as an independent investor and trader who works outside of finance, I've made  decent money trading stocks, ETFs, options, futures, forex, and cryptocurrencies (like Bitcoin and Ethereum.)I also have a number of long-term investments that have done well: some mutual funds, index funds, ETFs, and some individual stocks. (I still tell the story of getting in on the MasterCard IPO [initial public offering] as my greatest investment.)

Most of the gains I've made over the years, probably over 90% of them, have been made going LONG (bullish) on my investments. I'd say shorting/hedging has been a newer skill in my toolbox that I've used more in the last several years. But because I also trade options and futures, I've developed skills that allow me to take advantage of market volatility as well. (*It's very clean and direct to short the market with index futures.*)

So regardless of the storms I see coming, I'm generally upbeat on the American economy and our place in the world.

In this book I will refrain from discussing all things that were generally off-limits at our family Thanksgiving dinners: "No politics, no religion." Well, let me clarify: I will discuss the concept of political risk(s) in 2020, but not tread into the underlying bipartisan topics of those politics.

There are real issues in the US, UK, and

Europe. There are serious dynamics at play in the Middle East and the horn of eastern Africa, and there is drama in Asia: China, North Korea, and Hong Kong.

As I've already said, I'm not an economist, but I will say that North America and Asia, or specifically the United States and China —the dynamics between the two countries—is both an opportunity and a risk for investors in 2020, even before taking COVID-19 into consideration.

I'm an individual investor who manages his own money, and for a few members of my family, but I'm not a finance professional. I don't run a hedge fund. I don't sell a trader's newsletter, or have a huge following online waiting for my stock, options, or futures tips. I won't start a YouTube channel on trading. I'm just seeing things that I want to share with other investors. (I'll give you another example: I think the student loan debt in this country is out of control and could be the root cause of another housing-bubble-type situation.)

But like most investors, yourself included I bet, I just want to make sure that my family and I are safe, secure, and on the best financial footing for years to come: as my wife and I send our daughter off to college and we eventually begin a more leisurely lifestyle we like to call '*post-work.*' It's many years away for both of us, but I've never liked the *retirement* word. It sounds like a concept for very old people, and with our zest for life, learning, travel, creativity, and more, we'll never be that old!

I'm glad that I found a way to share these concepts with a broader audience than just my own circle of friends, family, and business associates. So thanks for listening to my ideas and for giving me a chance to show you what I'm seeing in the market. After that, it's up to you to do what you want with the information.

Another disclaimer reminder: Please remember to talk to your own advisors before making any changes in your own financial, investment, and/or retirement and wealth planning situation. Just remember: it's called 'personal finance' because your situation is most likely completely different than ours.

TWO

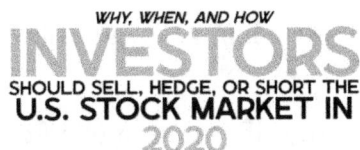

My Investing Education

HOW I GOT HERE

"The four most dangerous words in investing are: 'this time it's different.'"

- Sir John Templeton

Okay, a little background first... The first person to teach me about investing was my grandfather. He made money working for years at one of the big oil & gas companies in the US and worked his way up from a tough blue collar job to shift supervisor, and finally to a back office manager.

When he retired, after years of buying company stock and receiving stock options for even more, he was holding quite a bit of that company's dividend-paying shares in addition to a nice pension.

(By the way, if you're much too impatient right now to read about the lessons of Christopher the young trader, investor, and mogul-in-the-making, just move on to the next chapter. There we'll start the discussion about the headwinds in the market, and what I'll be doing about them and how I'll try to capitalize on knowing that they could be factors in our 2020 markets.)

Back to the story about my grandfather...

His advice to young Christopher (me!) about to invest all of my hard-earned savings was this:

> *"Individual investors almost always lose. But you don't have to..."*

For a few years, I accepted that lesson like a cautionary tale told by someone who was likely *burned* by an unforgiving stock market over the years.

But what I found out later was that my

grandfather was actually pretty sharp as an individual investor, and he did quite well with his various investments. Quite well. Enough to provide for his wife—my amazing grandmother—for the rest of her life, and to give my parents and their siblings a great start in life. He even left gifts for us, but I'll get to that in a moment.

Here is the rest of my grandfather's investing advice, shared with me over a period of several years before he passed away. I'm paraphrasing because to my knowledge, he never wrote them down. He never really claimed that they were all that unique or original; more like market truisms that he stood by.

But as he told me many times, if you've never thought about the collected wisdom from the past, you're doomed to make the same painful mistakes they did. And although there is nothing wrong with making your own mistakes, I'd prefer to avoid the quicksand.

Sure failure, losses, and mistakes build character, but for many, the early mistakes they make in money and investing are so devastating that they never recover.

So I wanted to learn from his experience, so very hard won. And over the years, I've seen similar echoes and confirmation of this generational advice in various finance books and interviews with some of the world's greatest investors, traders, and hedge fund managers that I know my grandfather was right.

Pieces of advice my grandfather had heard from others or learned along the way from his own wins (and losses) while trading and investing in the markets for many years:

- *If you take a profit, you've won. It's never a negative because you're better off than you were.*
- *You'll never perfectly time the top or the bottom, so stop trying.*
- *Always understand your investments. If not, get out.*
- *Read company annual reports and listen to their conference calls to get deeper insights into businesses and industries.*
- *Each day you continue to hold an investment is the same as repurchasing it. So ask yourself, would you?*
- *You can be right about an investment*

theory, but if you're early and you can't hold on, then you're wrong.
- *Watch trends, and try to ride waves, but don't be the last one to realize that the party's over.*
- *Cash is a viable investment strategy. And it also presents opportunities for you at critical inflection points.*
- *Try to watch price and market volumes closely because they signal institutional activity.*
- *Everyone has limited money to invest and everyone has limited attention or 'bandwidth' to worry about the investing choices they've made. Be very. very careful with both.*
- *Hope can never be an investment strategy.*

Like I said, using these lessons my grandfather did well with his money and his investments.

But in case you're concerned, that doesn't mean I was raised as a soft, pampered upper-class kid. Nope. Don't worry, you're not reading a book written by someone who was given everything in life. My siblings and I all went to public schools, then decent colleges (not Ivy) and I've worked hard all my life. I've made many of my own mistakes with money and I continue to learn every year. I also continue to read and study the markets, finance, and the various sectors of our global economy, and I have actively traded with my own capital earnings for years.

Nope. I didn't grow up with a trust fund, but my grandfather's investments did write a single check that paid for my college. (No students loans for this guy!) That was it. But it's still an amazing feat that my siblings and I and a few cousins are all college graduates, without any student loan debt, from a blue collar oil & gas technician's shrewd investments. Thanks, Grandpa!

THREE

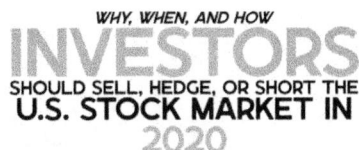

How This Book Is Organized

BEFORE WE GET STARTED

"An investment in knowledge pays the best interest."

- Benjamin Franklin

I want you, the reader, to see the factors that I see in the market and why I hear the stock market screaming for me to get out!

The general plan in this book is to show you the WHY of selling/shorting/hedging in 2020, the WHEN to take action based on some calendar-based strategies or possibly of signals present themselves, and the HOW to sell/short/hedge— outlining the various ways to make this preparation profitable with stocks, ETFs, options, and futures strategies.

- Why?
- When?
- How?

Let's discuss 'WHY'

As you read through this book, if you find yourself agreeing with certain risk factors in 2020 (outlined fully in the next chapter), then those are the ones you can watch for and also trade or hedge against.

Conversely, if there are others that you don't think will provide real headwinds to the markets, then you can simply ignore them. (i.e., My concerns about a higher education student loan debt bubble are not shared by a college professor friend of mine, for example. No harm, no foul. To each his/her own opinion.)

For example, some believe that with the long-term stability in the United States of America, any geopolitical risks around the globe only bolster and encourage investment here in our markets. There is some obvious truth to that. "The full faith and credit of the United States..." is respected across the globe.

However, I tend to think that there are some geopolitical factors (i.e., events, strife, drama) around the globe that will affect our 2020 markets, regardless of my deep sense of national pride, patriotism, and military service. (*Yes, I'm an honorably-discharged veteran who served in Iraq, but that's for another book.*)

Let's talk about 'WHEN'

As far as when any of these things happen, I'm definitely not a fortune teller, a modern-day Nostradamus, or a clairvoyant. So for some of these risks, I will likely create some protective positions when conditions are right (meaning cheap!) and for others, I will react as things develop. But I will say that COVID-19 is making the markets shudder. Here's another look at February 24, 2020, the Monday that the US markets realized that this virus is real and it's taken hold in Europe.

A sea of red in the US markets down on February 24, 2020.

But there's always a trading opportunity inside that fear. On that day, the biotech Gilead [ticker: GILD], the gold company Newmont Corp [ticker: NEM] and consumer goods company Clorox [ticker symbol: CLX], the maker of bleach were up on the day.

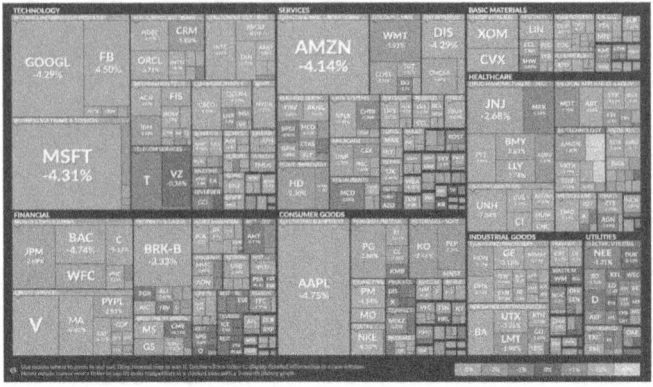

In different example of market pressure, if you believe that commodity prices are moving too high and that might give us an inflation scare, you could buy some PUT protection in the overall market (S&P500) on a rally day, when the indexes are all higher.

With options strategies, you might also do this with PUT spreads, or by selling CALL spreads above the market. We'll talk about this in HOW, but since options strategies are time-based investments, some consideration also has to be given to the WHEN, as in *when to initiate* these options positions.

Let's discuss 'HOW'

To me this is pretty interesting because over time, individual investors can gain more and more strategies (i.e., tools) to help them make money in the markets. For some this could just mean ETFs in addition to mutual funds. But for others, this could involve options, futures, or forex strategies to hedge your long positions. And in case you think derivatives (like options) are just a risky gamble, remember that Warren Buffett's Berkshire Hathaway makes serious gains by selling PUTS in indexes and in stocks he prefers like Coca-Cola [ticker symbol: KO].

When you're just starting out with a workplace retirement account, all your choices are generally long-based (bullish) mutual funds, or worse mutual funds in an annuity wrapper, one of the worst thing ever created, in my opinion. Their fees are high, creeping too close to 2% per year for fund managers and administrative overheads that spread their bets (I mean holdings) so wide, they're practically an index fund. But they can't give us those returns —beating or even matching an index because of the slippage that their fees take. Okay, rant over. You can tell my workplace retirement funds are reluctantly in index funds, even though I wish I could fully manage those assets NOW with my full service broker, and not way to roll them out when I retire.

But now, with options strategies, futures contracts, ETFs (the whole range of market, sector, specialized, and inverse), and even non-correlated assets, there are ways for individuals to profit in all market conditions. I'll explain a few of my go-to strategies in the HOW chapter.

FOUR

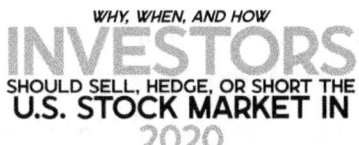
WHY, WHEN, AND HOW INVESTORS SHOULD SELL, HEDGE, OR SHORT THE U.S. STOCK MARKET IN 2020

The Why?

WHY SHOULD I GET OUT?

> *"One of the funny things about the stock market is that every time one person buys, another sells, and both think they are astute."*
>
> - William Feather

This chapter contains the headwinds that I'll be tracking this year that have the ability to send the market down. These range from systemic structural issues underlying the market to geopolitical concerns and more. If you ask me now what the number one risk is, I'd have to say Coronavirus COVID-19 is the one that keeps me up at night. It's the one that has sparked countless conversations with friends and family, and not to be insensitive to the potential human suffering and loss of life, I believe it's also the biggest risk for my family and our financial stability.

Here's My "WHY"

But if you think that the risk with this epidemic/pandemic is overblown, or believe it will quickly be handled by the world's top epidemiologists (I hope so too!), then why (else) should you sell your risk assets? Why should you hedge your long investments? Why you should potentially short the US stock markets?

Well, here's what I see right now as the significant headwinds to any continued bull market.

This is my current list of some of the risk factors for US investors/traders to consider in the 2020 trading year. Some of these will be outlined briefly below:

1. Wuhan Coronavirus; COVID-19
2. Tax Sellers in 2020
3. The REPO scare - repurchase liquidity
4. Earnings Weakness (EPS)
5. The American Political Climate
6. Geopolitical Factors (Brexit, the US Election, Impeachment, Iraq, Afghanistan, Iran, Syria, Hong Kong, Yemen, Saudi Arabia, Lebanon, Algeria)
7. The Long Run Up ('08 Housing, QE, and more) - "Didn't Take Our Pain"
8. Currency concerns
9. Global Slowdown
10. Global Trade War(s)
11. Looming $1.6T Student loan debt crisis
12. Environmental concerns
13. Technical indicators in the market
14. Opinions From Some People I Respect

Tax Sellers

The first reason to sell in 2020 is that many market participants may have been fooled by late 2019's market rally that took place because many of the sellers seemed to have just disappeared. They might believe that the lack of sellers in fourth quarter (November and December) 2019 was an indicator of the continued bullish sentiment of the market.

Why?

Because so many investors (individual and institutional) made serious gains in 2019's run up, I think many decided to wait to sell into the New Year to delay paying taxes for an additional year. With so many of 2019's capital gains carried into a new tax year, I believe many investors will be looking to lock in those gains, especially at the first sign of trouble. I want to get out before they do, especially the big whales!

The REPO Liquidity Scare

Overnight liquidity for banks, the repurchase agreements that spiked a couple times in 2019 (mid-September and December), and created a panic is a concern.

I believe this is a real warning shot for our financial markets in 2020. The spike to 8%/10% for repo rates (September), trading well outside the trading rates of 2-2.5%, was a warning and a surprise liquidity squeeze. Even at over 4% in December, it shows that this problem needs a more permanent solution.

The NY Fed's liquidity intervention helped normalize the repo rates, but there's already money in the system. Was it just the pressures of corporate tax day and those US Treasury bond auction settlements that removed all of that liquidity? Was it the Japanese holiday affected global assets in play? I don't really know if that explains it.

I'm no economist, just an individual investor trying to stay informed, but there's a warning here that looks like a flaw in the system. (Look no further than the Fed paying interest on idle bank reserves, a plan instituted only after 2008 and making this free money compete with financial system integrity.)

Watch for the Fed to also be challenged by an inflation scare in 2020 as commodities move.

If you don't know about this situation, I encourage you to read about it online. It should be discussed more often.

This REPO issue, and what the Fed does about it —especially if the markets react to a headline inflation number— is a reason to SELL, HEDGE, or SHORT in 2020.

Weakness of Earnings

Will earnings of US and global corporations be strong enough to hold this rally? That's the question everyone is asking in 2020.

I think the supply chain interruptions in China, plus Japan, and South Korea that are a side-effect of the COVID-19 outbreak have already added some serious dark clouds above many earnings estimates in a wide variety of sectors.

Nothing stalls, halts, or kills a rally faster than a poor earnings season, and I think that's what we have in store. And that means stocks are expensive... and risky.

SPY (NYSE)
SPDR S&P 500 ETF Trust

And if EPS (earnings per share) expectations don't hold up, then all of the smart investors (including you and me!) will reevaluate the P/E (price-to-earnings ration) we're paying for stocks.

As I write this the historical forward earnings multiple average for the S&P 500 is generally at 15 to 16, and we're at about 18. (Early 2019, it was 13.9, which is why many thought the market was cheap enough to buy.)

A high forward multiple is not enough reason to sell, but if too many companies—and the analysts tracking them—lower their earnings expectations, we could see a sell-off.

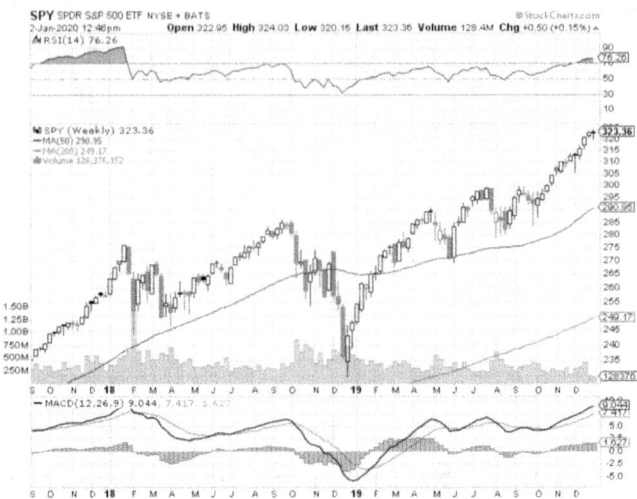

Compare this chart, the SPDR S&P 500 SPY ETF from January 2, 2020 with the next chart from late February.

Here is the SPDR S&P 500 SPY ETF chart from February 23, 2020. Notice the RSI at the top and the MACD crossover at the bottom.

The American Political Climate

As promised, my discussion of political topics will veer clear of any bipartisan commentary or editorial perspectives, but rather I'll just be mentioning things that I see that could have an impact on the US markets in 2020.

- The Democratic primaries
- The POTUS impeachment process
- The 2020 Presidential election (November)
- Ongoing investigations related to any US government officials
- General political divisiveness

As the Democrats in our two-party system in the United States prepare to choose a 'ticket' to run against the incumbent Republican president, the national polls (who's ahead, who is likely, etc.) tell a forward-looking story about the country and its outlook. When Wall Street determines that it doesn't like the profile of any of those forward-looking stories, there could be additional volatility.

The impeachment process in the U.S. Senate, of the American President, has already wrapped up and, as expected, was settled along party lines. Whether that has any lingering influence in 2020 remains to be seen, but it definitely contributes to the political divisiveness. Again, I could imagine scenarios where this continued division makes its impact on the economy, so it's a factor for me.

Lastly, I expect that the lead up to the US election to add some additional pressure on the markets, regardless of the assumed outcome. If the current administration stays, there is one implication for growth in our economy, but if another administration is elected, changes will come that may affect the regulatory environment for business, for example.

But what could turn out to be a complete wild card for the impact of the 2020 election is whether the COVID-19 Wuhan coronavirus takes hold in the US over the summer and fall and impacts the willingness of voters to go to the polls.

Yes, I know, I know... this is a wild concept and quite far-fetched at this point, but consider that millions of Chinese are under a mandatory lockdown right now and that seemed impossible to fathom even six months ago.

(This is a good place to tell you that many days during my commute, newscasters on my car radio often sounds like they're describing scenes from an edgy Hollywood movie. Yikes.)

Serious Geopolitical Risks in 2020

I can tell you that things like BREXIT, trade deals, and trade "wars," alongside threats of actual wars, the worldwide refugee crisis, and developing skirmishes, conflicts, and hostilities around the globe right now, all have the ability to impact the global stability in a way that would be felt in our financial markets.

On any given week, some of these geopolitical situations seem very important for the market and also security around the world in general. Many of these involve human tragedies on a global scale, and others are simply volatile dynamics between political powers, social forces, and more. Whether it's a single country, a humanitarian crisis, or a brewing war, these all the ability to move markets both in the US and abroad.

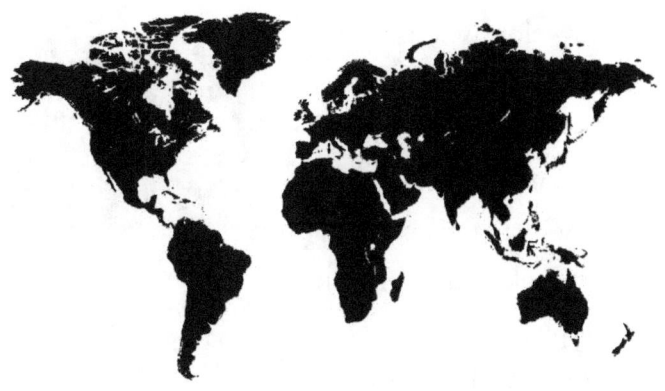

Technical Indicators of a Correction

In any market, there are a number of technical indicators that can potentially help traders and investors to know if the market is breaking down and will pull back.

Where can I see support and resistance? Are we range-bound? Will we be stuck in one area for an extended part of the year. (This is useful for selling options because time decay is your friend). Or are we actively trending, either bullish or bearish with this particular stock, ETF, or index?

It's beyond the scope of this book to explain all of the 'art and science' of using these indicators, but this list is a great starting point for assessing the market on your own terms. For some, just being able to study the candlestick charts closely, assessing the volume of selling vs. buying, and then marking out a few trend lines can be very instructive. Seeing what looks like recent envelope channels and support and resistance prices (crowd thinking!) can be useful.

An example of a candlestick chart, in this case without any moving average lines.

But be careful.

Technical indicators are not predictors of the future, and can obviously generate false signals. Why? Because what is being charted are the transactions of actual buyers and sellers on the ground who agreed on a price in that moment. It's just another way to view what has already happened, whether that was yesterday, last month, or sometime in the last year.

But be careful of *confirmation bias*, possibly the greatest problem with using technical indicators on your charts. Resist the temptation to simply find tools that support your current market, sector, ETF, or stock opinions, while ignoring others that contradict it.

Here are some technical indicators that I use,

and that you could consider adding to your toolbox in 2020:

- **Candlestick charting** (open, close, high, and low): This is one of the core parts of understanding the daily, weekly, and monthly charts. Buy or sell stocks based on candlestick activity and formations, rather than just fundamentals like P/E ratios, debt, book value, etc.
- **Relative Strength Index (RSI)**: With a range of 1 to 100, and RSI signal over 70 can signal that the stock/index is overbought, overvalued, or frothy, where an approach to 30 or below can indicate oversold conditions.
- **Envelope channels**
- **Trendlines** (support and resistance)
- **Bollinger Bands** (range of standard deviations)
- **MACD** - (Moving Average Convergence Divergence): Well-

known indicator based on changing distances between two exponential moving averages (26 and 12 EMA) with a reference signal line (9).
- **Ichimoku clouds** (or Ichimoku Kinko Hyo)
- **Supertrend indicator**
- **VWAP- Volume weighted average price**

If you use technicals. combining two or more indicators (like RSI and Supertrend, for example) might work for you, but don't bury your charts.

(This is a good place to recommend the site STOCKCHARTS dot com, which is a good place to explore indicators, outside of your brokerage account, and FinViz dot com for their screeners and heat maps that help you find information quickly by changing the way the data is presented. I also recommend the Options and Futures education at Tastytrade DOT com, and the interactive streams of traders and investors at StockTwits. I have no affiliation/referral relationship with these sites, I just think they're valuable. Check them out!)

Looming $1.6T Student Loan Debt Crisis

According to Forbes magazine, student loan debt in the US just hitting a record $1.6 Trillion. That average debt, carried by almost 45 million borrowers, is $32,731.

I can see a number of ways that this student loan debt creates a drag on our economy, especially if it seriously impacts other purchases like home buying, autos, etc., or the influx of college graduates don't get the employment that warrants the expense. Keep your eye on this topic, I think matters.

Opinions From Some People I Respect

I'd like to mention that there are others out there that I really respect that also talk about headwinds.

The first is Gary Vaynerchuk, the CEO of VaynerMedia, Inc (NYC, London, Los Angeles) and social media/web guru, who has said in several corporate keynote addresses that the United States never endured the real pain of the housing bubble, instead bailing ourselves out with free cash from the Fed. (Quantitative Easing

I, II, III, etc). He thinks that when we—i.e., the markets, the economy, venture capital, Silicon Valley—fall again, it will be an even harder landing, and Vaynerchuk believes that several big, well-known brands will likely go out of business. (He openly said that he plans to buy some failing brands—at firesale prices—to relaunch them into a new economy.) *You can easily find the sources of these statements and his other related comments on YouTube.*

There are others whose words of caution have helped me to form my own opinions about the risks of student loans, Brexit, and other topics. But again, do your own research about these topics, and watch for developments, to see if you believe they warrant inclusion on my list.

FIVE

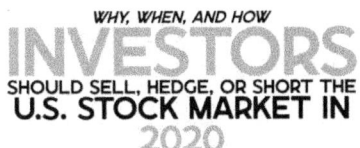

The When?

WHEN SHOULD I SELL, SHORT, OR HEDGE?

> *"The whole secret to winning big in the stock market is not to be right all the time, but to lose the least amount possible when you're wrong."*
>
> - William J. O'Neil

The first and most obvious time to sell, short, or hedge—directly taking on the question of when—is <u>immediately</u> because the many bearish factors mentioned in *Chapter 4: The Why* are already out there. As I already mentioned, the lack of selling in the markets in late 2019 could mean that many traders, investors, and institutions could be waiting until sometime early in the new year to liquidate their positions.

Why?

The S&P 500 was up almost 29% in 2019, the biggest single year gain since back in 2013. The Dow climbed over 22% in the year and the Nasdaq was up 35%. Sometimes when traders have big gains and don't want to take them in the current tax year, they'll carry them through the holidays and then look for an early exit into the new year. (Early could mean any point in the first quarter of 2020.) The trader psychology of not wanting to give back gains from 2019 could kick in pull the market down, because even the fund managers and institutional traders are still capable of having that 'fear.'

This process is the exact opposite of tax loss harvesting, when investors sell before December 31st to make sure they can take the tax loss on their next tax return.

If those sellers liquidate in early 2020, it could send those averages down quickly, perhaps after a typical *January Effect* push higher.

There is also the possibility that some will harvest their winners before April 15th in the US to make cash available to pay their tax obligations.

The January Effect

Depending on whom you ask, the basic concept behind the January effect is that many new investors put money in the market right at the beginning of the new year. These investors, some using their retirement funds, and others putting money to work in the new year, are often novices or at least less experienced with the markets. Some institutional investors will also make big trades just to get new positions opened for their holdings reports.

What's the psychology here that works against retail investors? After a strong 2019, a big start to January trading would give less-sophisticated investors a false sense of security that the uptrend will simply continue. "The water is fine, jump in!"

Coronavirus COVID-2019 Timetable

No one knows how the COVID-2019 outbreak will develop, but there are many factors which could dictate a schedule for traders in 2020:

- How well does containment hold outside Asia?
- When other companies (beyond Apple) start to report their own supply chain disruptions based on Chinese (Japanese, or South Korean) factory production
- When the COVID-19 virus is confirmed in places where it hasn't yet reached: the South American continent; the African continent (with the exception of a single case in Egypt, at this writing); and North Korea, for example
- When American society is affected broadly, possibly even to the level of widespread 'shelter-in-place' and social distancing orders (i.e., schools closed, college classes

cancelled/moved online, work suspended, etc.)
- And any other changes in the virus that create any level of serious concern in the general public (mutation, lack of dissipation in the summer months [as is widely predicted]; and more
- If market support and liquidity by central banks around the world fails to offset the continued selling a large institutional investors
- Other unseen factors...

Geopolitical Timetable

For events like trade wars, Brexit, conflict with Iran, Syrian refugees, and many other geopolitical problems/conflicts, and tension around the world, the only process that can help forecast when they might become a problem for our economy, a market sector, your stock holdings, etc., is to closely monitor them. Companies will often mention headwinds to their revenues and profits on their quarterly earnings calls and in their annual reports, so make sure you study those for your bigger positions.

For example, once you've identified a certain geopolitical situation that could negatively impact your holdings, or our market in general, then find ways to watch the news related to this factor. (I generally create 'Google search alerts" to get daily or weekly topics sent to my email inbox when I want to stay current on a topic without searching every day.

SIX

The How?

WHAT STRATEGIES SHOULD I USE?

> *"A lot of people with high IQs are terrible investors because they've got terrible temperaments. You need to keep raw, irrational emotion under control."*
>
> - Charlie Munger

This chapter is focused on the strategies that you can deploy once you agree on the 'why' and 'when' of selling your stocks. How can we both hedge our holdings—including against our long-term retirement accounts—and also profit from the downturns or increased volatility.

These will NOT be applicable to all people because finance is personal—that's why it's called personal finance! I don't know your immediate, current, and future needs, and regardless they're very likely different than my own. But regardless of your stage in life, you should be able to find something that will give you the edge once you see some downward pressure in the market indexes, your favorite stocks, or ETFs.

Short- and Medium-Term Spending Needs

The first category of investments is for any resources that you plan to spend over the next three to five years (for a car, house, condo, wedding, your kid's college, etc.) If you don't believe a bear market can last that long, it can. But the real factor is that even if a downturn resumes its

bullish trajectory in a year or two, how long will it take to earn back any losses (realized or unrealized.)

For short and medium-term expenses like those above, the HOW is clear:

- Just go into **CASH**. Or cash equivalents (i.e., money markets, certificates of deposit, etc.)
- The key here is to keep that money easily accessible, and without significant penalties to retrieve it.

Work-Based Retirement Plans

What to do about your retirement plans at work in a big sell-off? Even if you want to go short or hedge against a falling market, many retail investors have the issue of limited choice long-only mutual funds in their workplace retirement accounts (401k, 403b, or Roth IRAs).

I have this situation as well, and so does my wife, so for those assets we choose to either transfer some of the assets to their 'cash-reserve' investment choices to redeploy later or simply choose **index funds** (S&P 500, international, etc.) to  give yourself some dollar-cost-averaging the overall market during a prolonged downturn.

The general consensus with this sort of retirement-based investing is, of course, to not try to time the market. But since many mutual funds will underperform in a major sell-off, I'd rather not pay the high fees of a managed fund. Unless you're planning to retire immediately, it's probably better to go with index funds.

One last thing: Be very careful with going into all cash or money market funds inside a retirement account without doing some research on their *rebalancing and reallocating rules*. Why? Because some fund companies limit the percentage of funds that can be reinvested per transaction. For example, some plans maintain a limit of redeploying cash at only 20% at a time, with waiting periods in between. This restricts uninformed investors from cashing out at the top (or bottom), and waiting until they sense fear-ofmissing-out (FOMO), and reinvesting. Others plans have 'excessive trading rules' for mutual fund investors that move assets too often. Read your plan rules.

If it's your inclination to leave your workplace accounts alone, your tax-based investing and trading efforts should be focused on offsetting any losses or pullbacks in your 401k, 403b, or Roth IRA balances.

There are obviously many things you can do if the market starts heading down that lead to overall protection or short-term profits. If you're a little stubborn, like me, you might have positions or holdings that you don't plan on liquidating, no matter what the market does. You might even look for opportunities to buy additional shares at a discount, so some of these strategies are called **offset profits** that can help you make gains (on the side) to mitigate any unrealized losses you take inside your portfolio.

Looking at this another way, if you never plan to sell your holdings in Google's parent company, Alphabet, Inc. [ticker symbol: GOOGL], for example, you might focus your downside protection efforts on making money on the overall Nasdaq's  tech-heavy index using ETFs. In case you're still confused by all of the abbreviations, ETFs are exchange-traded funds, essentially mutuals funds (a 'basket' of stock holdings) that trade intraday on the market. Mutual funds set their price on market close.

Much of that depends on what your investments looks like and your investing timeframe.

If any of these trading strategies in this chapter are new to you, make sure to investigate the mechanics of the trades before you attempt execute them. Options and futures trades generally require extra permission from online brokers, so check the requirements on your trading or investing platform. Inside certain retirement accounts your choices will be limited (sadly).

Depending on your current situation, and the makeup of your portfolio, the most basic choices would be to sell any holdings you have that are at risk, locking in the gains, and consider shorting the same underlying security, sector ETF, or index from the same level.

Technology Stock: Trading Example Using ETFs and Options

Imagine that you see a signal in the Nasdaq, that makes you want to sell, short, or hedge your technology-based holdings.

Here are some examples of a few strategies available in a volatile market.

Imagine that you are holding shares in technology giant Oracle (ticker symbol: ORCL) which at the current market is trading about $54 and pays its shareholders a dividend of about 1.8% annually.

If you decide that should exit —or reduce— your hypothetical position in Oracle, then you could:

- Simply sell your holdings and move to cash.
- Liquidate your holdings and reverse from $54, where you short sell the

stock, buying it back later at a lower price to close out the trade.
- Sell the individual stock, and short the Nasdaq Index ETF.
- Sell the ORCL position and open option spreads in the index ETFs. For example, a bear call spread would include selling an at-the-money NASDAQ ETF call (ticker symbol: QQQ), and buying a call above that for protection. At about $214 per share at the time of this writing, the $214 strike price call a few months out would bring in about $69 in option premium and cost $2 for the $216 strike price hedge, for a total deposit into your account of $67, minus fees. If QQQ stays below $214 at expiration, you'll keep that money for each spread contract you write. A similar position would be a BULL put spread, where you buy a put and sell a lower one to partially offset your cost, but you'd need the QQQ to move into a specific spread range, before expiration, to make this

profitable. (Pssst: I strongly suggest you watch/read/learn everything you can about *option spread* trading, because it's a very powerful strategy to have in your tool belt, and it's hedged by design to limit your exposure.)
- You could research sector ETFs and inverse-ETFs on the Nasdaq and either buy them, making gains as the QQQ moves down, or build options strategies around these as well: selling a put and covered calls (both bullish on an inverse-ETF), or call and put spreads based on your outlook.

In this example, if you really want to hold your Oracle stock position, either because of the individual company outlook, the dividend, the sector, or some other factor, you could hedge with various easy-to-learn options strategies.

- You could **buy a PUT** below the

current price and a few months out to give you some downside protection. For example with ORCL at $54 now, the $52.50 PUT, three months out is quoted at about $161 (plus fees) for a single contract. Each contract would protect 100 shares from downside movements for 90 days, but then expire worthless. If the market, sector, or company pulls back hard before that point, you could sell your contract for a gain, using those funds to help you offset the unrealized losses on your underlying holding. (Just so you know again, buying options is <u>my least favorite</u> way to trade derivatives. I'd rather sell, that way option expiration dates and 'time decay' (sometimes referred to as *theta*) are on your side of the trade.

- You could also **sell a CALL** option on each one of your positions, also called **covered calls**. For each 100 shares you have you could sell one option contract, give yourself some downside protection. Because the strike price is based on volatility and time to expiration, a two or three month call contract could give you the most flexibility. If the stock is at $54 and you look out three months and sell a $55 CALL, you could take in (for this example) about $155 (minus fees.) If ORCL stays flat or drops in price, then you can keep this premium, plus any dividends. Of course, if the shares move up to $55, then you will make another $1 per share on your holdings, plus this premium ($155) and you would be obligated to sell. Either way, if you time it right, you might also collect your quarterly dividend as well ($0.24/per share.)

- Combining these two strategies, you could also sell a covered call above your stock current price (of course, dependent on your cost basis), and use those proceeds to nearly fund a protective put below the market price and out on the calendar.

Options Trading Strategies

> Remember options prices change with the volatility of the market, underlying asset price, and time left until expiration.

ETFs and Inverse-ETFs; Leveraged ETFs

Exchange-traded funds that move beyond market indexes and sectors have been created for all manner of trading. Be careful with these ETF, and their inverse versions, because they often don't have enough volume (liquidity) to make entries and exits all that simple. But for the ETFs, inverse-ETFs, or leveraged ETFs, applying conservative option selling strategies might give you hefty premiums to offset your holdings.

The leveraged ETFs from ProShares for example on the Nasdaq 100 come in a variety of flavors: Ultra QQQ, UltraPro QQQ, Short QQQ, UltraShort QQQ, UltraPro Short QQQ covering trades at 2X, 3X, -1X, -2X, and -3X the daily Nasdaq. But remember what my grandfather said: KNOW WHAT YOU'RE TRADING.

For me this means adding the most interesting and relevant of these ETFs (sector, inverse, or leveraged) and get to know how they trade and what to expect for average volumes in the ETF and underlying options.

Assets Not Correlated to US Markets

Another strategy that can be used to hedge against stock market losses is to find non-correlated assets. This is not for the faint of heart, but it disconnects your net worth from being tied to equity prices.

Many of these ideas may be more volatile than stock, ETF, and mutual fund investing, and obviously might not be suitable for all types of investors. These ideas are far and wide and will require more research that extends beyond the reach of this short book.

And liquidity is a big concern. If you buy a painting that you (and experts) believe will increase in value, it might take many years for that to be the case, and then you'd still need to find a buyer at that higher price.

Of course, it takes work to find investments that are not tied to US market moves. That said, some stocks like those dealing with consumer staples (food, clothing, etc.) might be at least partially immune to a massive selloff because those items will still be in need by shoppers, even if the country does some collective belt-tightening.

These include companies like Clorox (ticker symbol: CLX), JM Smucker (ticker symbol: SJM), Kellogg (ticker symbol: K), Kimberly-Clark (ticker symbol: KMB), PepsiCo (ticker symbol: PEP), Proctor & Gamble (ticker symbol: PG), and others. The strength of these stocks, and others like them, is that with their consistent dividend yields, many of the individual and institutional share owners are holding long-term for their quarterly payouts and in many cases will buy more shares if the cost of that yield gets too cheap.

Some traders put alcohol stocks like Diageo (ticker symbol: DEO)—with its well-known brands like Guinness, Johnnie Walker, Smirnoff, Captain Morgan, and Don Julio—and tobacco stocks like Altria (ticker symbol: MO) in this category as well, but I feel that these are perhaps too discretionary, and could lose sales if consumers have to make a choice between toothpaste and Vodka.

This line of thinking often leads investors to become interested in well-known market hedges like commodities (like gold, silver, oil, and natural gas), cannabis stocks (i.e., legalized marijuana), or cryptocurrencies like bitcoin [BTC], ethereum [ETH], litecoin [LTC], ripple [XRP]and other assets that they view as the polar opposite to the S&P 500. I've even seen discussions online of traders purchases music-related royalties, shares in a privately-held business, or the rights to ice cream royalties (Ben & Jerry's flavors).

You can certainly hold Comex Gold futures (symbol: GC), or one of the many ETFs related to gold like SPDR Gold Shares (ticker symbol: GLD), iShares Gold Trust (ticker symbol: IAU), Aberdeen Physical Swiss Gold (ticker symbol: SGOL), or physical gold, but remember you always need a buyer to be able to exit your trade.

I've traded Crude Oil futures (symbol: CL), BitCoin [BTC] and other assets in this category, but make sure you learn all you can even before you transfer you funds into those accounts.

SEVEN

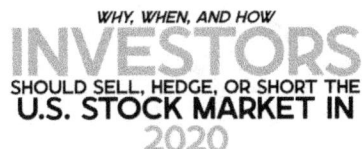

WHY, WHEN, AND HOW
INVESTORS
SHOULD SELL, HEDGE, OR SHORT THE
U.S. STOCK MARKET IN
2020

More Example Trades
COVERING OTHER POSSIBLE SCENARIOS

> *"Far more money has been lost by investors trying to anticipate corrections, than lost in the corrections themselves."*
>
> \- Peter Lynch

Before I show you a couple more hypothetical trades, I want to share a complex spread trade that I saw in the markets.

On February 21, 2020, SPY, the S&P500 ETF closed at $333.48, down $3.47, or (-1.03%). I noticed that the September PUTS between the $280 and $250 strike prices looked active and even had the appearance of a BEAR PUT SPREAD, also called a debit spread.

You can see (below) that on a down day in the market, these options were already up between 15 to 20 % on the day.

Puts for September 18, 2020

Contract Name	Last Trade Date	Strike	Last Price	Bid	Ask	Change	% Change	Volume	Open Interest	Implied Volatility
SPY200918P00250000	2020-02-21 3:50PM EST	250.00	1.82	1.70	1.81	+0.24	+15.18%	4,287	7,803	26.11%
SPY200918P00255000	2020-02-21 9:54AM EST	255.00	2.13	1.98	2.09	-0.48	-19.09%	350	11,732	25.54%
SPY200918P00260000	2020-02-21 3:34PM EST	260.00	2.48	2.29	2.41	+0.39	+18.66%	89	6,699	24.97%
SPY200918P00265000	2020-02-21 10:46AM EST	265.00	2.85	2.63	2.76	+0.32	+12.65%	4	5,795	24.37%
SPY200918P00268000	2020-02-19 3:10PM EST	268.00	2.39	2.87	3.00	0.00	-	6	267	24.03%
SPY200918P00269000	2020-02-07 9:41AM EST	269.00	2.97	2.95	3.08	0.00	-	1	0	23.91%
SPY200918P00270000	2020-02-21 4:14PM EST	270.00	3.11	3.03	3.17	+0.19	+6.51%	302	9,442	23.80%
SPY200918P00271000	2020-02-20 11:52AM EST	271.00	2.98	3.12	3.25	0.00	-	7	0	23.67%
SPY200918P00272000	2020-02-12 3:37PM EST	272.00	2.64	3.20	3.34	0.00	-	5	0	23.55%
SPY200918P00273000	2020-02-14 9:30AM EST	273.00	2.80	3.29	3.43	0.00	-	1	0	23.43%
SPY200918P00274000	2020-02-19 3:11PM EST	274.00	2.82	3.38	3.52	0.00	-	10	145	23.31%
SPY200918P00275000	2020-02-20 3:07PM EST	275.00	3.14	3.48	3.62	0.00	-	9	12,078	23.20%
SPY200918P00276000	2020-02-19 3:11PM EST	276.00	2.98	3.57	3.71	0.00	-	10	153	23.06%
SPY200918P00277000	2020-02-19 3:11PM EST	277.00	3.06	3.67	3.81	0.00	-	4	354	22.94%
SPY200918P00278000	2020-02-21 11:36AM EST	278.00	3.80	3.78	3.91	+0.64	+20.25%	5	293	22.82%
SPY200918P00279000	2020-02-03 10:07AM EST	279.00	4.93	3.88	4.02	0.00	-	4	0	22.71%
SPY200918P00280000	2020-02-21 3:43PM EST	280.00	4.33	3.99	4.13	+0.79	+22.32%	4,597	18,049	22.60%

Here are PUT prices at the close of trading for the SPY ETF for the SEP 18 2020 EXPIRATION on Friday, February 21, 2020.

The third from the left column is volume and with 4,597 contracts traded in the SEP $280 strike and 4,287 contracts traded in the SEP $250 strike, it looks like a BEAR PUT spread.

Here are the detail images:

Strike	Last Price	Bid	Ask	Change	% Change	Volume	Open Interest	Implied Volatility
280.00	4.33	3.99	4.13	+0.79	+22.32%	4,597	18,049	22.60%

This is the SEP 2020 SPY September PUT detail at the 280 strike price. (2/21/2020)

Strike	Last Price	Bid	Ask	Change	% Change	Volume	Open Interest	Implied Volatility
250.00	1.82	1.70	1.81	+0.24	+15.19%	4,287	7,803	26.11%

This is the SEP 2020 SPY September PUT detail at the 250 strike price. (2/21/2020)

Let's assume that a single institutional buyer had an order size of 4,250 contracts. (We can't know the details of the trade fully, so let's recreate it. For our purposes, we'll use the "LAST PRICE" numbers, in the fourth column from left.) So what did they likely trade?

- BUY-TO-OPEN 4,250 PUTS on SPY at the $280 STRIKE for SEP 2020 expiration at $4.33 ($433), for a total cost of $1,840,250, or $1.8M plus fees. They did this with SPY trading at around $333. To make it a spread trade, they simultaneous completed a SELL-TO-OPEN of 4,250 PUTS on SPY at the $250

STRIKE for SEP 2020 expiration at $1.82 ($182), for a collected total of $773,500. Total cost (and RISK) on the trade is $4.33 - $1.82 or $2.51 per option contract (controlling 100 shares) or $251: (approximately) $1,840,250 minus $773,500 which equals $1,066,750 (plus fees), or about $1.06M.

A couple things to note about this trade and its inherent strategy: This out-of-the-money spread is most profitable when SPY goes below $280 before/at September expiration, but stays above the $250 strike. With the price of the SPY ETF at $333 on Friday, 2/21/2020 down to the level of $280 [by September] requires a drop of seventeen percent (down -17.29%). By Monday, 2/24/20, the SPY ETF was already down -3.32%.

> The potential profit on a debit spread is to calculate the value of the spread minus what you paid, and minus fees.

Since the spread between $280 strike and

$250 strike is $30 and they paid $2.51 for this out-of-the-money trade, they stand to earn up to $27.49 optimally [minus fees] on each contract or $2749.

That $2,749 multiplied by the quantity of 4250 PUT spread contracts equals a full potential gain of $11,683,250 or $11.6M as long as SPY moves downward by September into this range. The full loss potential is the $1.06M debit.

What a trade!

And even if they don't wait for full profits, this is a tell that an institutional trader, hedge fund, etc., sees the downside risk/reward of betting against the S&P500 through the spring, summer, and fall of 2020. I didn't comb through all the expiration months on Friday 2/21/20 to find others possible trades like this, but this process could give you an indication of what others might be sensing in the market.

SPDR S&P 500 ETF Trust (SPY)
NYSEArca - Nasdaq Real Time Price. Currency in USD

322.42 -11.06 (-3.32%)
At close: 4:00PM EST

By 2/24/20, with SPY closing down at $322,

their trade already looks interesting. So here's another embedded strategy.

Since they paid $4.33 for the SEP $280 PUTS and they've already moved to $5.90 (last price) over the weekend and through Monday's trading day, it's possible that they could sell the debit PUTS for a $1.57 per contract gain or $157. With 4250 contracts in their spread, that would be a gain of $667,250.

If they sold the PUTS they purchased, the hedge puts they previously SOLD at $250 would now be their obligation to buy 4,250 contracts worth of SPY by Sep 2020 if it closes at or below $250. That's a huge (~$106M) obligation to buy 425K SPY shares (at $250), but it requires SPY to drop another 25% before that would be exercised. If SPY stays above $250.01 through September 2020 expiration, they'll keep the additional $773,500 premium from selling those $250 PUTS on Friday.

I doubt these savvy institutional traders would close this trade so quickly when the market has the potential to sell off quite a bit before Fall 2020, but it just shows that the spread can be taken apart and the PUTs that were sold below the trade can stand alone (if you have the capital) and be allowed to be exercised.

These are big numbers for individual traders but the underlying fundamentals are the same.

Other Trading Ideas in Down Markets

1. EARNINGS TRADES with Options: Watch for stock movement around earnings, especially if you believe that a company will underwhelm the markets. The increased volatility going into earnings could mean that selling spreads above and below the markets could be profitable. Just control your risk. Sound interesting? Then learn about *iron condors, calendar spreads, straddles, strangles, or iron butterflies* (options strategy), and the idea of selling spreads (calls and puts) above and below your underlying asset's market price at the same time, or across different expiration months.
2. PAIRS TRADES: Where you go

long and short on two securities at the same time that have some inverse correlation. (This is another advanced strategy, so do you homework!) For example, if you believe that the airplane manufacturing stocks could do okay, but the airline travel stocks will suffer, you could open a pairs trade with a LONG Boeing (ticker symbol: BA) and SHORT Southwest Airlines Co. (ticker symbol: LUV), for example.

3. TRADE LEAP CALENDAR Spreads with PUTs. How? Buy a long-term LEAP (long-term) put in an underlying security that you think might go lower. Because the asset is long-term, you'll pay a premium for such a far-off expiration date. To offset this cost, you can sell a closer (in time) put as a hedge and to lower your cost basis.

Here's an example:
If I believe that FedEx Corp [ticker symbol:

FDX] is overvalued and will pull back from its recent $154 price level, you could trade a leap spread with Puts. In February 2020, the JAN 2022 $110 PUTS have a recent price of $5.38 per contract or $538. In the near term, the APR 2020 $125 strike PUTS have a recent price of $1.19 per contract, or $119.

If you buy the JAN 2022 LEAP Puts in FDX, that option will gain in price as the underlying stock moves toward that strike price of $110, as long as it moves quicker than time decay. By selling the $125 Put for March 2020, you're temporarily obligating yourself to buy FDX below $125, but you're hedged by your leap if the stock goes to zero.

This example trade would cost $538 for the long-term Jan 2022 put - minus $119 (collected for selling the March 2020 put) totally a debit of $419. Assuming FDX stays flat or pulls back, but not more than down 18% by March 2020 (the difference of the current price $154 to your $125 obligation), then you could repeat the trade, reassess in the Spring, or close out the LEAP for a profit. If you repeat the trade, you'd want to check price levels again and decide the risk/reward of lowering your cost basis again.

EIGHT

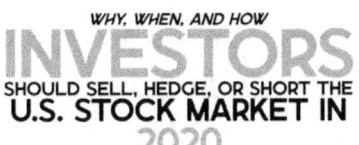

WHY, WHEN, AND HOW
INVESTORS
SHOULD SELL, HEDGE, OR SHORT THE
U.S. STOCK MARKET IN
2020

Final Thoughts

ALWAYS REMEMBER WHY YOU'RE INVESTING

> *"Look at market fluctuations as your friend rather than your enemy. Profit from folly rather than participate in it."*
>
> \- Warren Buffett

Although there are a lot of strategies include here with a large number of potential market sectors to look at, as an individual trader/investor it's perfectly reasonable to limit your focus:

- Choose one or two sectors, indexes, or stocks to target your short-selling or options trading
- Consider what you're actually holding or hedge only against those assets
- Stay broad with market index trades only
- Limit your trading strategies to a small toolbox of things you can do, or learn to do well - i.e., options (i.e., put spreads, covered calls, etc), futures (i.e. morning pre-market /ES E-mini trades, etc.), shorting (gapping stocks, earnings class, etc), inverse ETF trades, earnings trades, calendar spreads, etc.

If you can become proficient at a few trading setups and strategies, it will be enough to not only hedge your way through 2020, or even better, have a profitable trading year because you catch the downside moves and capitalize on the increased market volatility when market moves get more aggressive.

Never expect to be successful on every trade

or investment, but control your risk, and protect your capital. This is why discipline is key and understanding your own trading psychology is so powerful. (*I use a trading log and investing journal for stocks, options, forex, and futures:* this one!) so that when the market is closed I can look back on my trades and reassess my progress. I don't just review my brokerage statements. I want to remember my thinking in the moment I entered the trade or the investment.)

Good luck out there. And always stay nimble with your money, your investments, and your assets. (And never forget that going to (or staying in) cash is always an option.)

One of your number one assets going forward is your accumulated investment knowledge, so do what you can to stay informed, but always consider your sources.

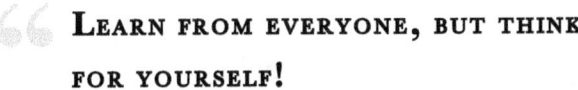 **LEARN FROM EVERYONE, BUT THINK FOR YOURSELF!**

Look at trading strategies, understand headline economic data, and listen to the respected trading veterans in finance.

I always watch what the crowd does —its buying and selling patterns—and try to understand the underlying market psychology, as much as I  can. But remember that the big whales like institutional investors—and the programmed algorithmic trading & quants—move the markets, not small fries like you and me. It's okay to not have the same level of market research, tools, and indicators that they have. Just stay nimble.

As I said before, I'm not a perma-bear and don't consider myself a contrarian. I think you can get pretty chopped up always betting against the crowd. So you don't have to be an *automatic contrarian* either, but "don't be the last one to realize that the party's over."

Always remember who and what you're building wealth for:

- You and your loved ones
- Your overall financial freedom and independence

- The ability to travel (anywhere, anytime…)
- Your comfortable home(s)
- Other family expenses (weddings, college, and more)
- Hobbies, passions, and interests
- Your charitable causes and giving
- Helping your community and
- Income security in your retirement

It's an important list.

Good luck and have a safe, happy, healthy, and prosperous 2020. Thank you again for reading my short book and considering my perspectives. I hope it helps you in some way. - C.W.

Acknowledgments

Special thanks to Eli Rutledge for the cover art, typography, and book layout in the ebook and paperback editions. Also special thanks to Louis Hansel for the map image on the 'World of Finance' page. I appreciate my early beta readers and my editor (A.T.) and their amazing feedback. A.T. helped me quite a bit, but she was still too shy about her contributions and didn't want to be listed in my book. Any errors and typos that remain after their help are entirely of my own doing. I owe all of you lunch!

Author's Notes

THANKS AGAIN FOR READING THIS BOOK. This **author's notes** section is my way to share a little bit of the process behind this project.

From the start, I was aiming for this:

> "**A timely personal finance book for a "toppy" market.**"

Some version of that tagline became my "elevator pitch" whenever I would tell people what I was working on. It helped me organize my thoughts, keep focused, and ultimately finish. But I sincerely was not prepared for the emotional ups and downs of this journey—even for this relatively short book.

It's definitely more work to write a book than I ever imagined because of the pure psychology of getting the words down. During the writing process, the workload either felt like #1 or #2:

1. "I can do this...simple, straightforward, easy-peasy. I'll just share my thoughts about money, personal finance, and the markets, using my broad experiences as an individual trader and investor, and once I'm in the zone, I'm sure the ideas will just pour out of me." [...or this...}
2. "Okay, wow, this writing-a-book stuff is hard. Well, not hard, but definitely tricky. Everything I write could really use an extended explanation, some qualifying remarks, or at least some thoughts about why I bothered to include the topic in this text. But I'm not writing a finance textbook for classroom use, so I don't need to explain every little thing I mention."

But of course, the other real shocker were these December 2019/January 2020 revelations about a viral outbreak in the city of Wuhan, China, presumably from an animal wet market.

Now, as I finish this text in late February, that outbreak has grown into possibly the most significant headwind for U.S. and global financial markets for the rest of 2020 and beyond. During the revising stage and final edits of my project, this shifting global landscape affected by the outbreak (epidemic > pandemic) made its way into almost every chapter included here.

China, South Korea, Japan, Italy, Singapore, Hong Kong, Iran, Thailand, and the United States are all facing great containment battles with many other countries right behind them. <u>*These are obviously serious public health concerns, but also threaten the economic stability across the entire planet.*</u>

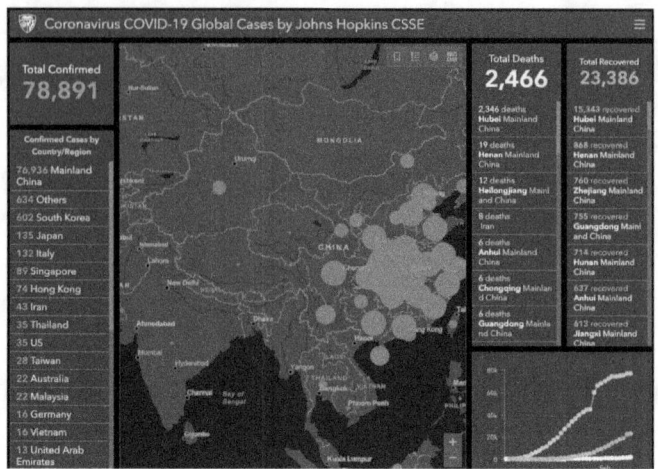

COVID-19 Coronavirus data from Johns Hopkins University, accessed on Sunday, February 23, 2020, 11:34am.

Author's Notes

Two days later: COVID-19 Coronavirus data from Johns Hopkins University, accessed on Tuesday, February 25, 2020, 9:45am.

As a father, husband, son, and brother, neighbor, world citizen, I'm really saddened by the loss of life from this outbreak to date, and very concerned about the real losses going forward — all across the globe. Protect your families, your loved ones, and your future, but also help each other whenever you can.

Be safe out there.
-C.W.

About the Author

CHRISTOPHER WESTFIELD is an individual investor and trader, father, and husband who taught himself most of what he knows about trading and investing stocks, ETFs, options, futures, forex, and  cryptocurrency. (His hard-working grandfather taught him the rest!) Born in rural Connecticut, Chris has lived in Seattle, Boston, Munich, Atlanta, and Memphis, but has spent most of his adult life in the Chicago area where he now lives with his wife and daughter. He works at a cool startup during the day (hey team!), and continues to learn more about personal finance, trading, and investing every day as his *'relentless passion.'* This is his first book with *PiggyBankMedia*.

Thank you so much for reading this book. Please consider leaving an honest review wherever you found it.

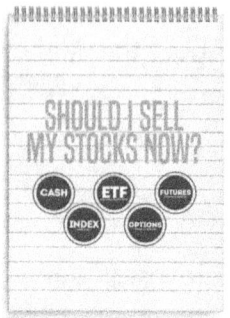

NOTES

STRATEGIES